The Uncanny Of Life

Tania

BookLeaf
Publishing

India | USA | UK

Made with ❤ on the BookLeaf Publishing Platform
www.bookleafpub.in
www.bookleafpub.com

Dedication

*To my **FARISHTA** (my Guardian Angel)*
who has made me felt different.

Preface

There are many events that occur in your life without giving any prior signs and symbols. Life turns upside down and you just can't stop figuring out .

Your pastlife Karmas and your present life lessons take a toll on your living , yet you choose to rise and shine , and accept life with open arms .

Acknowledgements

I would like to thank **GOD** (Mera Farishta), **The Universe** and **my family** for their unwavering support throughout the journey.

A special thanks to **Shivaaye** (Mahadev). My this life is **ALL YOURS** in everyway.

Heartfelt thanks to **BookLeaf Publishing** for creating such an incredible platform for the writers who just only like to keep their thoughts restricted to their inner hearts but not anymore.

I also extend my gratitude to my readers who embark on this journey with me , thank you for living an unpredictable lovely life in your imagination with me.

Love Love Lovingly

Listening to their stories
forming your own fairies
later turning it into unexpected glories..

Life is hard
Life is tough
Let's not forget,
it is extremely rough...

But what matters is
How you face this thing called fate
How you hold on to your mate
even when there is no scope
Let's not dull the hope
Hold tightly to the rope
Don't let it go
Don't give up

Love comes only once

Flourish it gently
Move with it smoothly
Love it lovingly ...

Maybe

Maybe life has humbled me so much
That I don't hate or love anything as such..

Peace is the only craved feeling
That I miss it's touch
Don't wanna rush
Never wanna create fuss
Just wanna have a bitter sweet brush
Filled with core inner feelings
Breaking barriers
Making a new crush
Wanna shine and blush ...

Maybe you are never on a wrong track
Maybe it's just an unexpected turn
That take you far away
Where you can easily burn ...
And of course from where you never wanna return
Coz there are your favorable lessons that you learn

And that's the life you definitely wanna earn..

Patience is the true virtue
That adds up to your value
You may act like a statue
That's the trick to rescue
Moving ahead without any clue
Hoping to fix things with your glue
Just to contend the feeling of blue....

Sometimes mistakes cannot be forgotten
Healed wounds again are opened
Wow!! What an irony of life
Some guardian angels are only seasoned
Your heart ache ,
Your feelings get hurt ,
Your emotions get no air to breathe
Maybe everything works when it is only licensed...

Everyone has to choose a Path

After all everyone has to choose a path
And walk a mile
Keep a smile
Has to frame a style
A strange number to dial
And sometimes it is so hostile......

What a cage
So fierce rage
Can't skip this page
Coz this is gonna bring the change.....

Needs to be firm
Has to reset the definition of this living term
Will surely earn
And get my fair share of turn...

YOU v/s YOU

When you are not done yet,
When you fail to understand yourself,
When you fail to take stand for your words,
When you lose control over your emotions,
When you end up not obeying your responsibilities,
When you don't wanna face the reality anymore,
When you wanna give up pretending everything,
When nothing seems right,
When you wanna run away,
JUST UNDERSTAND
YOU HAVE LOST YOU.

Everyday is a new war

Everyday is a new war
A part of me wants to hide in a bar.
Everyone tries to juggle
With their fantasy bubble.

Live...Hustle.. Laugh ... is a craft
But still there is something that is saved in a draft.
Run as fast as you can
But then you have to stop when it puts a ban.

An emerging lifestyle gives us an insight-
How to shine bright....
Have faith and keep moving with a flow,
Until it brings real joy and glow.

There is no rise without a fall

Behaviour forms a pattern
That is just like a ring of Saturn.
Living needs to be lived
Just like a cheesy dip.

Every growth needs to be embraced
To walk against that rat race.
Believe in your deeds
That is the way to lead.

Walk along the flow,
Your destination will give you glow.
You are perfect and whole,
There is no rising without fall.

Won't let it Break

Life is a journey where you meet plethora of people.
Some of them become an unexpected part of your life
That they always try to make your happiness triple.

Ups and downs bring an exotic version of you out,
Where one tries to amend and other shouts.
No conversation for many years....
Suddenly pops up a notification that you don't want it to
disappear.
Was the unknown bond too strong? Or were you took it
wrong!!!
Life gave another chance to rectify the mistake...
How can you let go of a friend
who has always been there for you even when you were
not awake.

Unaware in the past,
Don't wanna walk fast..
Gonna bake our own flavoured cake
And definitely won't let it break.

Life is short, so as Time

Always be there for the ones who are in the darkness....
What if you wanna help but they don't wanna tell!
What if you wanna be there but they don't want you to
care !
What if you don't want them to be a sufferer
but they don't want you to be settler!

Life is short so as time.
Don't let them do any crime.

Trynna being Happy is a new trend
Everyone wants to buy this brand.
Don't think too much
It's only gonna you crunch.

Forever is a lie
Life itself is a cry
Don't let urself fry
Fly in your own free sky.

DREAMS...

Well Dreams do come true...
The ones too you don't even know are a part of your
dreaming...

Life shifts like everything is creaming
Don't know why is it all brimming !!!!

But still something is missing
Of course that shit is pissing ....
Beyond having everything,
yet the cloud is sneezing
Why all of this is breezing
Where time is squeezing !!!

10. No Feelings yet full of Feelings

Having no feelings is a good feeling though...

From everything to nothing
and nothing to everything
The journey is about to sink
in front of your eye and its blink

Letting everything go
Like you are ready to blow
With a new form of show

Wow! Life is so uncertain
But don't worry ,
You enjoy your keratin

The consequences of being numb or being in pain
Are just merely a vain
Let the emotions rain
Let them sweep away with this moving train

Isn't it better to have a no feeling at all
Bcz it's a good feeling to call......

Hard to Understand Ourselves

Lga tha shayad sab theek hai
But in this heart shayad sab freezy hai

Why does it become so hard to understand ourselves
Dil hai deemag nhi that works on shelves

Yeah I know I get anxiety
But yehi toh hai aane wale khoobsurat kal ki security...

Ups and downs
Tears and laughters
Sab draw hota chla jata hai just like crafters ...

My unspoken words are way too shant mere andar
Bt shayad meri silence hi bchaati hai hone se kuch
blunder

I know you are worried about me

But kya kru...
My life is not that easy
Coz this is a different wali rose bushes tea...

Somewhere Everywhere

Somewhere everywhere
We are poles apart,
yet I love the way we care...

Somehow here and there
We always move around each other like a flair....

Somewhat here and somewhat there
We always spread into each other's lives like a flare .....

Yes...
Somewhere everywhere
We are there for one another
who helps to climb the success and struggle stair......

Everything happens for a reason

After all
Life is to accept it
Live it and
Learn from it...

Why is it hard to accept
and it becomes the only theft??

Why is it Good
as it is made of wood...

Why is it bad
but still you are glad!!!

Remember everything happens for a reason
And that reason is always good
Just feels like getting free from a prison.

Let's take oath

Not to waste any cloth.
Held your head high
And take a relief with its sigh.
You are so strong
You won't let anything happen wrong.

Whatever comes you way
Mend it, Welcome it
By giving it your life pay.

After all
Life is to accept it
Live it and
Learn from it...

But your Existence could be

Not all changes are positive,
but your smile could be....

Thinking it all over from bottom to top
What would it be?

From drowning to frowning
From howling to growling
This is what it should be....

You might not be positive
but your existence could be ....

Your Universe is bigger than You

Don't stop
You have to make it to the top...

Your growth awaits you
Don't leave it incomplete like a clue....

Enjoy your emotions while controlling them
Transform into a blooming gem....

Turn your gaze inwards
It's time to move forward and onwards....

Give yourself the permission to lean on your soul crew
Just have your own brew....

No one can decide for you
Your universe is bigger than you
Enjoy this version of you
And become a new you....

Dear Kith and Kins

Kith and Kins
Why are you holding sharp edged pins?
Are you not afraid to pay after party bills?
Or do you rely on safety pills?

Have some chills
and focus on your frills....

Dear Kith and Kins
This is my loudest call ,
as it is my own will and
I don't want you to step in my grill...

Oh my lovely kith and kins
Don't try to compete with my chin!!!!

Hustle, Fight and Shine Bright

Hardships never define you
They define your strength to struggle

Right or wrong is just an illusion
It only puts you in confusion

Need to stand firm
Live life on your term

Expecting things to be in your favour
is just like hurting your lover

Understanding and accepting is an art
You just have to settle your heart

Hustle, fight and shine bright
Let people be wrong about you and
keep them out of your sight...

Seeing yourself glowing is such a delight
Wow! What a life......

Who are you?

Broken???
Well that's a symbol of strength.

Healing???
Well that's a symbol of your patience and its length

Giver???
Well that's a symbol of a true being and a great friend.

You are a human full of experiences and
you definitely know how and when to bend...

No vibrations are to be send
You are you,
Your perspective is not supposed to be lend!!!!

I wish to be....

I wish to be You
To know who are you...

I wish to be the Genie
To fulfill your dreams and
repair your deepest scars...

I wish to be the Healer
To dig deep into you and
throw your sorrows far...

I wish to be your Soul Energy
To cleanse your depth and
take you to the Mars...

Would you???

Would you still love me mate???
If I disappear, would you really wait???

Crossing the woods alone
Trynna understand myself
but
Where will I find the key?
Where is my favorite cup of tea?
Why do I always look at you in a glee?

Oh dearie mate....
Why are you so mysterious
just like the depth of the sea???

Gratitude is Magnificent

Being blessed is a blessing
What a bliss of The Universe
Taking care of each miracle
Gratitude is magnificent
Positivity is the real scent
Life is an affordable rent
There is so much to spend
Give your hand to lend
But don't bend
Enjoy this trend
Let the end role to be played at the end.....